OFF THE RIM

Thoughts and Observations
of the Game

By

SANDY SPIN SLADE

— *Spinsational Publishing* —

Published by Spinsational Publishing
2276 Griffin Way Suite #105
Corona, CA 91719

Book Design and Production:
White Light Publishing, Huntington Beach, CA
Illustration: Felix Morales

Publisher's Cataloging in Publications
(Prepared by Quality Books Inc.)

Slade, Sandy.
    Off the rim— : thoughts and observations of the game / by Sandy
"Spin" Slade.
        p. cm.
    ISBN 0-9645906-0-3

    1. Basketball—Juvenile literature. 2. Achievement
motivation —Juvenile literature. I. Title.

GV885.2.S53 1995   796.323
                                    QBI95-20200

This book is dedicated to my parents,
Dan and Phyllis Slade.
It was their constant love and support
that guided me to believe
that anything in life is possible.

Basketball and Life

Sometimes in life you will need to take a timeout.
Shooting is trying to succeed with your hopes,
dreams, and wishes.
A foul is when somebody takes advantage of you
and pulls you down.
But a free throw is taking advantage of an easy
opportunity.
A pass is giving someone else a chance.
The last second shot is risking everything you have
made for yourself.
As you get older and wiser you enter into overtime.
Who wins shows that they have given it their all
and succeeded.
The handshake at the end shows the "REAL"
winner and loser.

By: Brandy Noice
1/15/95
Eighth Grade
Royal Palm Middle School
Phoenix, Arizona

Introduction

Growing up on a small farm in Northern Wisconsin, basketball was an important part of my life. My parents realized and encouraged this so much that my Dad made it a priority to lay down a basketball court before remodeling our old farm house.

My brothers and I spent thousands and thousands of hours on that court, through all kinds of weather.

Chopping through the layers of ice and snow in early Spring to get "on the court" as soon as possible was a yearly tradition. This wasn't a chore, but a desire—a desire to play the game we loved so much. Even though this court is long gone now, the memories of learning the game will always be there. As I look back at where it all began, I reflect on all the experiences I've had, and realize each experience has had an impact on not only my skills, but my approach toward life.

Whether it was playing high school ball in front of 50 people, attending basketball camps since age 11, playing Division I basketball at Fresno State University, or performing in front of thousands at an NBA playoff game at Chicago Stadium, I've learned something from each and every experience.

Off the Rim was first written for the kids who attended my clinics. I wanted to leave them with something they could refer back to long after the clinic was over. The few suggestions I wrote down quickly turned into dozens, and I thought that instead of just sharing these observations with a few, why not share it with all who would be interested. The reflections expressed, albeit simplistic, are meant to reinforce and remind.

I encourage you to add your own thoughts and observations as well, and include them in the blank pages provided in the back of the book. Write any thoughts you feel are important to you.

I wish you continued success as you challenge yourself to not only become a better basketball player, but to become a better person.

— *Sandy "Spin" Slade*

The only limitations that exist
are the ones we put on ourselves.

—

Every time you step to the free throw line
go through the same motions—
establish a ritual.

—

Whenever a teammate does something well
on or off the court,
let him or her know.

In practice, with permission
from your coach, switch positions—
guards be posts, posts be guards.
This will create a respect for
each other's positions.

Free throws are FREE.
A player does not get many chances for
an uncontested shot in a game.
Make the most of the opportunity.

Always be the first person ready for practice.

—

Never believe there is such a thing as an "impossibility".

—

When practicing alone,
turn on your favorite music—
it will motivate you.

When you think that you've learned all
there is to know about the game of basketball,
you're through.

—

To increase your hand and forearm strength,
sit down and dribble low,
alternating one finger at a time.

—

Have motivational music playing
when your team runs out on the floor
for pregame warm-ups.

Remember, the most expensive basketball shoes do not automatically make a great basketball player.

The first shots you take when you step out on the court are close to the basket. As you warm up, begin to increase your range.

—

Whether you're shooting or passing the ball, follow through every time.

—

Watch basketball games on television—you can learn a lot from observing others—good and bad.

*Concentrating
means remembering
to do things
correctly the
first time.*

Strong individuals accept blame,
rather than blaming others.

—

If you are not practicing,
you can be sure that your competition is.

—

Always do the right thing—
that way you won't waste energy trying
to correct your mistakes.

A dedicated person follows his/her own beliefs,
not everyone else's.

—

A champion isn't always the winner.

—

When putting on your basketball shoes,
put the first shoe on the same foot
every time.

*Before every practice
and every game,
set a personal goal
for yourself—
a goal that
no one else needs
to know about.*

When you practice alone,
work as hard as if your coach was
there watching.

—

Repetition is the key.
Repetition breeds confidence and
confidence equals success.

—

A winner is a dreamer who just won't quit.

Rent and watch the movie **Rudy**.

Luck is a direct result of
preparation meeting opportunity.
Be prepared.

Ask yourself
after every practice and every game,
*"Did I do the best that I possibly could
have done today?"*

Get a good night's rest
the evening prior to competition.

—

When you pass the ball to a teammate,
pass it the way you would
like to receive it.

—

Eat pasta for pregame meals.

*Don't ever let
anyone convince you
that you're too
short, too slow or
not talented enough.
Success comes from
the size of your
heart.*

Complete every drill.
You hurt only yourself if you quit
before you're done with the drill.

—

Do not savor a victory until
the final buzzer has sounded.

—

Dress appropriately before each game.
What you wear is both a reflection of you
and your team.

Remember,
playing the game of basketball
is only temporary—
getting a good education
will last a lifetime.

Don't be too hard on yourself.
Sometimes self-criticism can be more
harmful than good.

—

Respect your coach.

—

Make time to work on your defense
outside of "team" practice.

*During a game,
the role of a substitute
is not only to support his
or her team out on the floor,
but to mentally prepare
to enter the game
at any time.*

Surround yourself with positive people.
Don't make time for complainers.

—

The game of basketball is all about intensity.
Strive to maintain consistency.

—

Be a good listener.

Remember,
people who criticize are not content until
they bring you down to their level.

—

A key reason why teams are beaten is
that they allow themselves to think
that they can be beaten.

—

When practicing alone,
challenge yourself constantly
by developing game-like situations.

*Remember,
two basketballs
can fit through the basket
at one time.
You only
have to put
one in.*

Whenever you set a goal for yourself,
make sure it is achievable,
yet challenging.

—

Don't shy away from a more skilled player—
take on the challenge.

—

Great players are made during the off-season—
stay in shape.

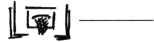

The style of your play on the floor
says a lot about your personality.

Appreciate your fans.

Know what you want to do with the ball
before you receive it.

Keep your feet moving at all times.

Always take a shower
after every practice and game—
you don't want to catch a cold.

Have fun!

Butterflies
before a game
are good—
they give you
an edge.

Don't wear jewelry
during practices or games.

—

Don't challenge a referee's decision.

—

Warm up properly before you practice—
this reduces the chance of injury.

*Talk
is cheap—
action
says it all.*

Always wear two pairs of athletic socks.

When you receive the basketball,
immediately put the ball in
the triple-threat position—
this allows you the quickest opportunity
to shoot, pass, or dribble.

*No one is
ever too tall
to learn how
to dribble
the basketball
well.*

Always square up to the basket
when you receive a pass.

Wear high top basketball shoes
or have your ankles taped
before every practice or game—
this reduces the chance of
an ankle injury.

Try to attend at least one
basketball camp per year.

Girls, whenever you have a chance,
play in a pick-up game with guys—
they make you play harder.

—

Every person on the team should take turns
sweeping the floor before practice.

—

Own your own basketball.

Imagine yourself
doing well—
and
you will.

Treat your teammates as you would like
to be treated.

—

Never underestimate the talent
of your opponent.

—

Save all newspaper clippings about your team—
not just the ones that mention you.

*Substance abuse
has no place in life.*

Remember, basketball is a team game;
every person on the team is an important part.

—

Use the restroom just before the game.

—

Listen to your father's advice.
He may have knowledge about the game
that you are not aware of.

Listen to your mother's advice.
She may have knowledge and insight about
the game which you are not aware of.

Ω

If you knock down your
opponent during a game,
help them up.

Ω

Shake hands with the opponent,
including their coach,
after every game.

*Kids are always
looking up to you,
imitating and watching
every move—
conduct yourself
accordingly.*

After every game, take the time to
reflect on how you played that night.
What things did you do well?
What things could have been improved upon?

As a team,
find ways to make extra money
so that you can participate in tournaments
that your school normally
could not afford.

When practicing free throws,
only count the ones that are made
without touching the rim—
challenge yourself.

⌐

Learn how to play the game *Beat The Pro*.

⌐

Never say, *"I can't."*

When receiving a pass,
have your hands up
to show your teammates that
you want the ball.

—

Accept compliments graciously.

—

Read *They Call Me Coach*
by John Wooden.

Do not make the excuse that you can't practice because there are no indoor courts available. Find an outdoor court.

Give your coach your full attention.
There is nothing more frustrating for a coach
than to have players not listening
when he/she is speaking.

—

Post players,
whenever you receive the ball in the paint,
keep the ball up—
make the most of your height.

—

Take care of your uniform.

If you are going through a personal problem,
talk to your coach.
If you're not comfortable talking to your coach,
find someone else to confide in.

—

Always be the last person to leave
the floor after practice.

—

Don't chew gum
during practice or games.

Stretch together as a team
at the beginning and
at the end of practice.

—

Learn to jump rope.

—

Every time you take a jump shot,
have equal weight on both feet,
with your dominant foot slightly forward.

There are appropriate times to use "flashy" moves— don't just use them to bring attention to yourself.

When you shoot the basketball,
aim at the hole of the basket;
not the front or back of the rim.

—

The place to make mistakes is in practice.
Don't be afraid to try new drills that
your coach asks of you.

—

Learn to spin the basketball.
It develops hand/eye coordination.

Remember,
even if you are not one of the starting five,
you are equally as important to
the success of the team.

If you must fly to an away game,
make sure you carry
your uniform and basketball shoes
on the plane with you.
You don't want to show up
without your equipment.

*Don't carry the burden
of your team's
success or failures
on your shoulders—
each individual
is equally
responsible.*

Mental imagery is key
in executing the proper fundamentals.
Clearly imagine success
and you will attain success.

—

Don't wear your good basketball
shoes outside.

—

Choose a role model carefully—
sometimes individuals are not
who they appear to be.

*Don't ever
talk back
to your
coach.*

Be serious in your warm-up.
The intensity will carry over into the game.

—

Whenever a time-out is called during a game,
run, don't walk,
to the bench.

—

Whenever your coach blows his/her whistle,
run, don't walk,
to the next drill.

If anyone does something nice for your team,
send him/her a thank-you note
from the whole team.

—

Never sit down in practice
unless your coach tells you to.

—

Learn your school song.

*Sometimes
things may not go
the way you would
like them to.
How you handle
adversity
is a reflection of
your character.*

Do not skip school the day after a long road trip.
Dedication and discipline must be carried out
when you're a part of a team.

Some days you just can't buy a basket.
Make it up on the defensive end.
There is no excuse for playing bad defense.

When shooting a jump shot,
the majority of the power comes from the legs,
not the arms.

—

Whenever your coach is speaking,
get in the habit of holding the basketball
in the triple-threat position.

—

Mental toughness is defined as
maintaining composure
under all sorts of adversity.

The image you portray
is a reflection of you, your team,
and the school you represent.

—

Talking about a teammate
behind his/her back
causes dissension on the team.
Keep your comments
to yourself.

—

Create a team cheer
and use it.

One of your goals
should not be concentrating
on maintaining your scoring average,
but concentrating
on what your role is
for overall team success.

—

Keep your uniform shirt tucked in.

—

Wear wristbands.

Smile a lot—
it's
contagious.

A great player
is one who is willing to practice alone
those drills which aren't fun.

—

Learn to juggle.
This develops hand/ eye coordination.

—

Remember,
water breaks are determined by the coach
during practice.

*At the beginning
of the season,
set team goals.
These goals
should be posted
in the locker room
so that everyone
can be reminded
of the task
at hand.*

Don't quit the team
just because you do not
like the way your coach operates.
You'll come to regret this decision.
You'll feel much better about yourself
if you "hang" in there.

—

Try to get your school pep band
to play at all your home games.
It livens up both the crowd
and the team.

Sometimes
your season may not go
the way you would like.
This is when you dig down deep
and just keep going.

If you work hard enough
to receive a full-ride scholarship
to play basketball in college,
do not take it for granted.

Being fast is associated with speed;
quickness is associated with reaction time.
Strive to develop both.

—

Inspiration
comes from watching
or listening to others.
Motivation
comes from within.

—

Have the *National Anthem* played
at all of your home games.

During a game,
don't wave
to your parents or friends
in the stands—
there is plenty of time
to visit with them
after
the game.

Concentrate on your studies—
if you don't make the grades,
you won't play.

—

When playing away,
treat the home-school property
the way you would like your
own school's property treated.

—

Volunteer your time
to help out a youth basketball league.

During a game,
there are always a lot of people
stating their opinion.
The only person
you should be listening to
is your coach.

The purpose of a time-out
is to go over game strategy,
not to have personal conversations.

*Don't be
the type of person
who looks back
at his/her life
thinking,
"I wish I would of
done this or that."
Take calculated risks
and live life
completely.*

Dear Athlete and Coach:

Humorous and learning experiences pertaining to basketball are always worth sharing. If you would like to share your stories with other readers, please write and tell me all about them.

Take care.

Sandy "Spin" Slade
2276 Griffin Way
Suite #105
Corona, CA 91719
FAX (909) 279-3957

— *About the Author* —

Sandy "Spin" Slade *is considered by many to be the best basketball handler in the world today. Sandy's enthusiasm, creativity and athletic ability create spectacular performances revolved around spinning basketballs and ball-handling techniques. Sandy's shows have been enthusiastically received at NBA and college half-times, school assemblies, camps, clinics, and corporation conventions. Additionally, Sandy's* ***Spinning and Winning Clinics*** *are held throughout the country for the purpose of improving the basketball skills of young players and exposing them to sure-fire formulas for personal improvement. Sandy is a positive and dynamic role model for everyone with whom she comes in contact. Her energy and commitment to excellence are contagious!*

Notes

Notes

. . . .
. . . .
. . . .
. . . .
. . . .
. . . .
. . . .
. . . .
. . . .
. . . .
. . . .
. . . .
. . . .
. . . .
. . . .
. . . .
. . . .

Notes

. . . .
. . . .
. . . .
. . . .
. . . .
. . . .
. . . .
. . . .
. . . .
. . . .
. . . .
. . . .
. . . .
. . . .
. . . .
. . . .
. . . .

Share your insight...

Now that you've enjoyed "words of wisdom" which inspire and motivate your game, why not pass this book on to your team? **Better yet**, get extra copies by clipping and mailing the handy order form below. You can **SAVE $2.00 or more** by ordering more than one copy!

Spinsational Publishing
2276 Griffin Way, Suite #105-126
Corona, CA 91719
(909) 279-3476
FAX (909) 279-3957

☑ **YES!** Send me extra copies of *Off the Rim*. If I'm not completely satisfied, I can return any copy for a full refund.

Send one copy for $5.95	

Or, SAVE $2.00 or more by ordering 2 copies or more:

Send ____ copies at just $4.95 each	
Shipping $1.50 first book, plus .50 each additional	
CA Residents add 7.75% sales tax	
Payment Enclosed (check or money order)	

Please Print:

Name_____

Address _____

City _____

State_____   Zip _____

☐ Please send me information explaining how I can get **Sandy "Spin" Slade** to appear at our school, camp, or special event.

☐ Please send me information explaining how I can have a **Spinning and Winning Basketball Fundamentals Clinic** at my school.

Spinsational Publishing
2276 Griffin Way, Suite #105-126
Corona, CA 91719

— Make checks payable to Spinsational Publishing —

Share your insight...

Now that you've enjoyed "words of wisdom" which inspire and motivate your game, why not pass this book on to your team? **Better yet**, get extra copies by clipping and mailing the handy order form below. You can **SAVE $2.00 or more** by ordering more than one copy!

Spinsational Publishing
2276 Griffin Way, Suite #105-126
Corona, CA 91719
(909) 279-3476
FAX (909) 279-3957

☑ **YES!** Send me extra copies of *Off the Rim*. If I'm not completely satisfied, I can return any copy for a full refund.

Send one copy for $5.95	

Or, SAVE $2.00 or more by ordering 2 copies or more:

Send _____ copies at just $4.95 each	
Shipping $1.50 first book, plus .50 each additional	
CA Residents add 7.75% sales tax	
Payment Enclosed (check or money order)	

Please Print:

Name_____

Address _____

City _____

State_____   Zip _____

❑ Please send me information explaining how I can get **Sandy "Spin" Slade** to appear at our school, camp, or special event.

❑ Please send me information explaining how I can have a **Spinning and Winning Basketball Fundamentals Clinic** at my school.

Spinsational Publishing
2276 Griffin Way, Suite #105-126
Corona, CA 91719

— Make checks payable to Spinsational Publishing —